MYTHOLOGY OF THE WORLD

THEMES OF WORLD MYTHOLOGY

by Rebecca van den Ham

BrightPoint Press

San Diego, CA

© 2023 BrightPoint Press
an imprint of ReferencePoint Press, Inc.
Printed in the United States

For more information, contact:
BrightPoint Press
PO Box 27779
San Diego, CA 92198
www.BrightPointPress.com

ALL RIGHTS RESERVED.

No part of this work covered by the copyright hereon may be reproduced or used in any form or by any means—graphic, electronic, or mechanical, including photocopying, recording, taping, web distribution, or information storage retrieval systems—without the written permission of the publisher.

LIBRARY OF CONGRESS CATALOGING-IN-PUBLICATION DATA

Name: Van den Ham, Rebecca, author.
Title: Themes of World Mythology / by Rebecca van den Ham.
Description: San Diego, CA: BrightPoint Press, 2023 | Series: Mythology of the World |
  Includes bibliographical references and index. | Audience: Grades 7–9
Identifiers: ISBN 9781678205003 (hardcover) | ISBN 9781678205010 (eBook)
The complete Library of Congress record is available at www.loc.gov.

CONTENTS

AT A GLANCE	4
INTRODUCTION UTNAPISHTIM'S FLOOD	6
CHAPTER ONE COMMON THEMES IN CREATION STORIES	12
CHAPTER TWO TRICKSTERS	22
CHAPTER THREE THE HERO'S JOURNEY	32
CHAPTER FOUR DEATH AND THE AFTERLIFE	46
Glossary	58
Source Notes	59
For Further Research	60
Index	62
Image Credits	63
About the Author	64

AT A GLANCE

- Myths are stories that explain the workings of the world. They have been told and retold for many centuries.

- Themes are patterns found in myths and other stories.

- The theme of creation is common in myths from around the world. People want to know where they came from.

- Most creation stories begin with gods or the world being created from nothing.

- Trickster characters are popular in myths. They make people laugh because they refuse to follow any rules.

- Some trickster characters are hated for hurting humans. Others are loved because they help humans.

- Heroes are important characters in many myths. They inspire people to do great things.

- A hero's journey can be divided into three stages. Each stage has several steps the hero must complete.

- Most cultures tell stories about what happens when people die.

- Some myths tell how people can prepare for the afterlife. Doing good deeds while they are still alive is another common theme in these myths.

INTRODUCTION

UTNAPISHTIM'S FLOOD

Enlil was the ruler of the gods. He thought that humans were too noisy. He wanted to kill them with a flood. But another god named Ea loved humans. Ea warned a man named Utnapishtim (oot-nuh-PISH-tim) about the flood. Ea helped him make a plan.

Utnapishtim built an **ark**. He filled it with other humans and animals. He loaded the ark with food and supplies.

Utnapishtim brought many people and animals aboard his ark. He hoped to save them from the flood.

The storm was so strong that it frightened even the gods. It raged for six days and nights. The rain stopped on the seventh day. The sun came out.

The ark rested on Mount Nisir. But Utnapishtim didn't know if the land was dry. He sent out two birds. Both came back. He then sent one more. It did not come back. This told Utnapishtim that the third bird found dry land. He released all the animals.

Enlil was impressed that Utnapishtim had survived. The god decided to reward him. He granted **immortality** to Utnapishtim and his wife.

Utnapishtim did not know if it was safe to leave the ark after the storm. He sent out birds in search of dry land.

This myth is from ancient Sumer. This civilization was in the Middle East. The story was part of a poem called the *Epic of Gilgamesh*. Flood myths are told all over the world. This myth also has the theme of rebirth. The world Utnapishtim knew was destroyed. But a new world was born.

WHAT ARE MYTHS?

Myths are the world's oldest stories. They explained how people thought the world worked. Many myths are still told today.

Themes are ideas that readers can find in works of literature. Many myths share the same themes. One story may contain several themes. Some themes are more common than others. Well-known themes include the creation of the world, characters

Myths can have many themes. One of the most common themes is the creation of the world.

who like to cause problems, how to be a hero, and what happens after death.

1
COMMON THEMES IN CREATION STORIES

Since ancient times, people have wondered how the world was created. No one knows for sure how it happened. Myths from many cultures aim to explain this mystery.

Readers often see common patterns in creation stories. Order is brought from

chaos. This vast emptiness is often represented as water. The earth and people are then created.

CREATION FROM NOTHING

A Chinese myth said that the world began with a cloud shaped like an egg. When the

The god Pangu helped create the world. When he died, his body turned into the mountains, the sun, and the moon.

egg cracked open, a giant god came out. His name was Pangu. The cloud's lighter vapors floated upward. They became the heavens. The heavier vapors sank down. They turned into the earth. Pangu pushed them apart so they would not mix again. Pangu grew every day for 18,000 years. All this growing exhausted him. He laid

ROOTS IN RELIGION

Most myths started as part of a culture's religion. People in ancient times worshiped many of the gods and goddesses in these stories. Although many cultures had similar myths, the details of the mythology and religions differed in many ways.

down and died. Pangu's body became the mountains, the sun, and the moon.

In ancient Japan, creation began with soundless chaos. The gods appeared and had children. Izanami and her brother Izanagi were two of these children. They went to the end of the Bridge of Heaven. It led to a formless and watery area. Izanami and Izanagi stirred the waters with a jeweled spear. When they pulled it out, drops of water formed an island. Izanami and Izanagi kept creating together. They made all the islands of Japan.

CREATION FROM DISMEMBERMENT

In some creation myths, the world is made from a god's body. These myths help people think about the life cycle. Things are born. They then die. But new life is always growing.

A Norse myth tells the story of Ymir (EE-meer), the first being. When the world began to form, there were two parts. One place was hot and fiery. The other was cold and icy. Ymir was a giant who appeared in the Great Gap between them.

The first man and woman came out of Ymir's armpits. They had children. The god

Ymir's murder was a gruesome one. It is said that so much blood spilled from the giant's body that it drowned nearly all the other giants.

Odin and his two brothers were some of them. When Ymir turned evil, Odin and his brothers killed him. From his body parts, they made land where people could live.

A Brazilian tribe told a myth about an armadillo named Daiiru. This animal species still lives in Brazil today.

Ymir's flesh became the land. His skull was the sky. His brains turned into the clouds.

FROM UNDERGROUND AND UNDERWATER

A tribe in Brazil told the story of the god Karusakaibö (koo-roo-sa-KI-bo). Daiiru was an **armadillo** who served as the god's helper. Daiiru found humans while burrowing underground. He helped Karusakaibö make a rope. They lowered it into a hole so the people could climb out. This myth explains how people came to live in the world.

The Polynesian god Maui created the Hawaiian Islands. It all started when he wanted to show his older brothers that he could catch the biggest fish. W.D. Westervelt authored books about Hawaiian history. He wrote, "It is said that Maui was not a very good fisherman."[1] His brothers would not give him any bait. Maui cut himself to solve the problem. He rubbed blood from his wound on a magical fishhook. He then tossed it into the ocean. Maui thought he hooked a giant fish. He told his brothers to row with all their strength. When they did, they dragged

After Maui dragged up the Hawaiian islands, he tried to join them into one with his fishing line. But he pulled too hard and broke them into even more pieces.

up land from the bottom of the ocean. It

became the Hawaiian Islands.

# 2

TRICKSTERS

Tricksters show up as a popular theme in myths from around the world. Tricksters are often smart and sneaky. Many of them can transform into objects or animals.

One famous trickster is China's Sun Wukong. He was a vain and greedy monkey. But the other animals loved him for his joy and curiosity. The other monkeys made him their king.

China's Monkey King had many adventures. Although he had some bad qualities, he became a beloved character of mythology.

Growth is a major theme in the myth about Monkey. He eventually moved past his greed and vanity.

The Monkey King wanted to live forever. He had many adventures while trying to achieve immortality. For example, a holy man taught Sun Wukong to fly. The Monkey King also learned to change himself into seventy-two different trees, animals, and insects.

Sun Wukong wanted a weapon as important as he felt he was. He stole the Dragon King's treasured iron rod. Professor Haiwang Yuan wrote, "Able to expand or shrink at his command, the iron rod becomes the monkey's favorite weapon."[2] Sun Wukong shrunk the rod and placed it behind his ear.

The Jade Emperor brought Sun Wukong to heaven to keep him out of trouble. He gave Sun Wukong a job cleaning the stables. But the Monkey King decided this job was beneath him. The emperor then gave him the job of guarding the Garden of the Immortal Peaches. These special fruits gave the gods wisdom and immortality. Sun Wukong ate many of the peaches. He hoped they would make him immortal. But he made a big mess with them.

    The mess angered the gods. They sent soldiers to kill Sun Wukong. But he fought them with his iron rod after increasing its size. He lived to have more adventures and eventually grew out of his vanity and greed.

    The Monkey King is a symbol of human growth. People may be vain or selfish. But they can grow through their experiences.

People who read about Sun Wukong may see different sides of themselves in him.

MISCHIEF AND MORE

Tricksters get away with all kinds of mischief. Sometimes they cause trouble.

WHY DO PEOPLE LIKE TRICKSTERS?

People are drawn to tricksters because they are often entertaining characters. Trickster gods do things people only wish they could do. Sometimes people enjoy it when tricksters get in trouble for their mischief. Hearing these stories often makes people laugh.

Anansi risked his life to give stories to the world. He even captured the leopard that Nyame wanted.

But humans sometimes benefit from a trickster's actions.

Anansi is a trickster of West African mythology. The Ashanti tribe told stories about him. One myth told how Anansi gave people storytelling. People were bored and restless. The sky god Nyame had a wooden box that contained all the world's stories. Anansi thought buying the box would solve this problem. But Nyame told Anansi the price was more than he could pay.

Nyame wanted a python, a leopard, hornets, and an invisible fairy. Any of these creatures could easily kill Anansi. But Anansi tricked them all into being captured. He exchanged them for Nyame's wooden box. Literature professor David Leeming said that Anansi "paid the price so that the people would have stories to tell for ever."[3]

STEALING FIRE FOR MANKIND

Many tricksters are beloved by fans of myths. Some tricksters teach humans skills, such as hunting or playing musical instruments. Many cultures have a story of a trickster bringing fire to humans. The trickster usually steals the fire first.

The Mazatec people of ancient Mexico told this type of myth. An old woman gathered fire as it fell from the stars. But she kept it all to herself. **Opossum** offered to get the fire for the rest of the people. In exchange, he made them promise never to eat him. Opossum pretended he was cold.

The opossum also appears in myths from Central American cultures. In these stories the trickster often escapes danger by using its intelligence.

The old woman believed him. She let him get close to the fire. He then grabbed it with his tail. He ran and ran, sharing the fire with everyone he encountered. Opossum's close contact with the fire also explains why these animals have bald tails today.

3
THE HERO'S JOURNEY

Heroism is another common theme in myths. Heroes are often strong, brave, and humble. They put others' needs ahead of their own. Heroes can also inspire people to help others. Professor David Leeming wrote, "To study the hero is to gaze into a mirror."[4]

Hero stories have been popular for centuries. They have even inspired writers of today to make up new hero stories. Comics and movies about superheroes are examples of these modern myths.

The hero's journey is a common theme in mythology. It has also become a part of many modern stories.

STEPS OF THE HERO'S JOURNEY

Often, a hero goes on a quest. This theme is sometimes called the hero's journey. Joseph Campbell was a professor of world mythology. He also wrote about the hero's journey. He divided it into three stages. Each stage has many steps. Most hero stories follow this pattern. But not every hero matches every step.

In the first stage, the hero prepares for the quest. Usually something happens to give him a push. Most heroes are men. But Psyche was a woman. Her story is from ancient Greece. Psyche loved her husband.

Joseph Campbell spent much of his life studying myths. He broke the hero's journey into stages to help readers understand it better.

But she thought he was a monster. One night she discovered he was really the handsome god Eros. His mother Aphrodite was against the marriage. She hid Eros from Psyche. Psyche's quest was to find her husband. But first, she had to complete a difficult task.

Aphrodite was convinced Psyche could not accomplish the task the goddess had assigned her. But a gift from Demeter helped Psyche get it done in time.

Aphrodite led Psyche to a huge pile of mixed grains. She told Psyche to sort them by morning. Helpers often appear in myths to give the hero special tools. The goddess Demeter sent ants to Psyche. They helped her sort the grains. The goddess Persephone also wanted to help Psyche find her husband. She gave Psyche a golden box. But she told Psyche not to open it. Psyche took it with her as she searched for Eros.

Many heroes must leave behind everything they know. No one knows when they will return. In some myths, their families give them up for dead. Psyche's family thought her monster husband had killed her.

In the second stage of the hero's journey, the hero faces trials. There may be temptation to do something wrong. For instance, Psyche became curious about her box. When she looked inside, the contents put her into a deep sleep. She almost died. But Eros found her and woke

SIMILAR THEMES

Professor Joseph Campbell studied myths in the 1900s. He discovered that many civilizations used the same themes in their myths. He was amazed by the similarities. The details varied. But many myths even seemed to tell the same story.

her. By the end of this stage, the hero has accomplished something important. Some heroes are granted rewards for completing their quests. Psyche was made immortal for completing hers.

In the third stage, the hero goes home. Often, the hero returns as a champion. Psyche triumphed against Aphrodite when she reunited with Eros. Journalist Philip Chrysopoulos wrote, "Today, the myth of Psyche and Eros still symbolizes the search for personal growth through learning—as well as true love."[5]

PERSEUS'S JOURNEY

The ancient Greek myth of Perseus is another example of the hero's journey. An evil king wanted to marry Perseus's mother. Perseus tried to stop the marriage. The king wanted to get rid of Perseus. He sent Perseus on a deadly journey to kill Medusa. She was a monster with snakes for hair. One look at her turned people to stone. Everyone thought Perseus would be killed. Many others had failed at this task.

The god Hermes gave Perseus winged shoes. They helped him fly. Hermes also told Perseus to go see the three Gray

Perseus put the tools given to him to good use. He used them to find and kill Medusa.

Sisters. They only had one eye among them. They took turns seeing with it. Perseus snatched it. He agreed to give it back only after they told him how to find Medusa.

The ancient Greeks saw Perseus in a constellation. The group of stars shows the hero holding his sword in one hand and Medusa's head in the other.

Soon, Perseus met the goddess Athena. Author Rick Riordan retold Perseus's myth in a modern book. He wrote that Athena knew "some day a great hero would come along—someone worthy of ending Medusa's curse."[6] The goddess gave Perseus a mirrored shield, a sword, and a bag. These tools would help him defeat the monster.

When Perseus found Medusa, he only looked at her in the mirror. This kept him from turning to stone. He then chopped off her head with the sword. He put the head safely in the bag. Perseus had to run away from Medusa's sisters. They wanted to kill him for what he had done. But Perseus escaped.

THE HERO'S JOURNEY

Stage 1
The hero prepares for a quest. Something pushes the hero to do this. The hero must leave home and everything familiar.

Stage 2
The hero faces trials. They often include temptation to do a wrong thing. If successful, the hero may receive a reward.

Stage 3
The hero returns home, often a champion. The hero is changed by the experience. Personal growth is a common result.

There are three basic stages to the hero's journey. Although the details vary, the basic pattern remains the same in all myths about heroes.

Perseus still needed to save his mother from the wicked king. He used Medusa's head to turn the king to stone. He then needed to dispose of the head. He gave it to Athena. Kelly Macguire writes about ancient history and mythology. She said the goddess placed Medusa's head in the center of her shield "to terrify her enemies."[7] Later, the Greek gods made Perseus a **constellation**. He lived forever as a picture in the night sky.

4
DEATH AND THE AFTERLIFE

Most cultures have stories about death. Some myths explain what happens after people die. Some offer comfort to those left behind. Other stories are meant to prepare a person for the afterlife.

A JOURNEY TO THE UNDERWORLD

Many myths talk about an underground land of the dead. It is often called the underworld. This location may have been

The National Museum of Anthropology in Mexico displays a disk of the Aztec underworld god.

chosen because so many cultures bury their dead in the ground. Many cultures tell stories of a hero who visits the underworld. A story from Mexico shows this kind of hero's journey. Heroes make these journeys to help humans. Helping humans is a common theme in underworld myths.

The ancient Aztecs called the underworld Mictlan. Quetzalcóatl (KET-sahl-KOH-ah-tul) was this civilization's god of knowledge and wisdom. He went to Mictlan to get the sacred bones. The gods needed them to create humans. Quetzalcóatl had to pass through nine regions of Mictlan. Each was

Quetzalcóatl was said to look fierce. He is often shown as a feathered serpent.

more dangerous than the last. He crossed over a huge river and rocks as sharp as razors.

Quetzalcóatl almost froze to death. Strong winds nearly blew him away. He made it past arrows. He even faced jaguars.

At last, Quetzalcóatl reached the ninth region. He asked for the sacred bones. But the underworld god did not want to give them up. He tried to trick Quetzalcóatl. The god asked him to make music by blowing

MYTHS OF QUETZALCÓATL'S EXIT

Quetzalcóatl was the king of Tula. But the god of the sky expelled him from this ancient capital. In one myth, he left on a raft made of snakes and disappeared beyond the horizon. In another myth, he set himself on fire. He then turned into the planet Venus.

into a shell. But there was no hole. The shell could not make sound without one. Quetzalcóatl picked up some worms. They ate a hole through the shell.

    The underworld god would still not give up the bones. Quetzalcóatl grabbed them and ran away. Bats chased Quetzalcóatl until he fell into a deep hole. The underworld god thought Quetzalcóatl was dead. But Quetzalcóatl climbed out of the hole and made the long journey to earth. He used the bones and his own blood to create the Aztec people.

JUDGMENT OF THE DEAD

Some myths show that one's deeds in life matter. Doing lots of good things before death earns a person or god a better afterlife. Other myths describe more than one place for the dead. Dying in battle may take people to one afterlife. A high status in society might take people to another. Some cultures even have special places for children and mothers.

Owen Jarus writes about history. He said, "The ancient Egyptians . . . believed that the dead could reach a paradise of sorts, where they could live forever."[8]

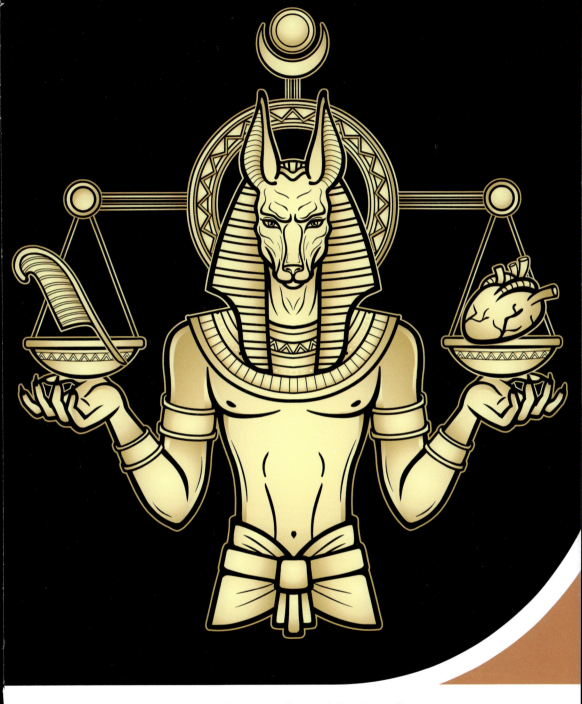

The ancient Egyptians believed that souls were judged in the afterlife. Only souls that were light with good deeds went on to a pleasant afterlife.

But their souls had to be judged first. The dead journeyed down a river by boat. They arrived at the throne of Osiris. He was the god of the underworld. The hearts of the dead were weighed on scales. Some hearts were heavy with sins. A monster ate these souls. Other hearts were light with good deeds. These souls went on to a heavenly afterlife.

THE END OF THE WORLD

Some cultures have myths that foretell the end of the world. The Norse stories named the end of the world Ragnarok. Signs of

Norse mythology stated that there would be signs of Ragnarok. They included three cruel winters with no summers between them.

In Norse mythology, the end of the world happens in Ragnarok. But a new world begins when the battle is over.

this event would include wars, plagues, and earthquakes. People would stop obeying laws. Winter would last for three years. After this, many evil monsters would get loose. The gods would fight against them. But the gods would all die in the large battle. Only a few of their children would be left. One human couple would also survive. After Ragnarok, the world would start over again.

    Myths have many layers. They also have many meanings. Thinking about a myth's themes helps to discover its meanings. Creation, tricksters, heroes, and the afterlife are just some of the themes found in these exciting stories. There are many other themes, too. Focusing on themes leads to a deeper understanding and respect for both life and myths.

GLOSSARY

ark

a gigantic boat

armadillo

a mammal with very thick skin that lives in North and South America

chaos

disorder and confusion

constellation

a group of stars that makes a shape connected to a story

immortality

the ability to live forever

opossum

a mammal about the size of a cat that lives in North and South America; it has no fur on its tail

SOURCE NOTES

CHAPTER ONE: COMMON THEMES IN CREATION STORIES

1. W.D. Westervelt, "Legends of Maui: A Demigod of Polynesia and of His Mother Hina," *Internet Archive*, 1910. https://archive.org.

CHAPTER TWO: TRICKSTERS

2. Haiwang Yuan, "Monkey King," *Western Kentucky University*, March 20, 2004. https://people.wku.edu.

3. David A. Leeming, *The Handy Mythology Answer Book*. Detroit, MI: Visible Ink Press, 2015, p. 340.

CHAPTER THREE: THE HERO'S JOURNEY

4. David A. Leeming, *The Handy Mythology Answer Book*. Detroit, MI: Visible Ink Press, 2015, p. 282.

5. Philip Chrysopoulos, "Eros and Psyche: The Greatest Love Story in Greek Mythology," *Greek Reporter*, February 14, 2022. https://greekreporter.com.

6. Rick Riordan, *Percy Jackson's Greek Heroes*. New York: Disney-Hyperion, 2015, p. 28.

7. Kelly Macguire, "Medusa," *World Mythology*, June 14, 2022. www.worldhistory.org.

CHAPTER FOUR: DEATH AND THE AFTERLIFE

8. Owen Jarus, "Ancient Egypt: History, Dynasties, Religion and Writing," *Live Science*, December 15, 2021. www.livescience.com.

FOR FURTHER RESEARCH

BOOKS

Zachary Hamby, *Introduction to Mythology for Kids: Legendary Stories from Around the World*. Berkeley, CA: Rockridge Press, 2020.

Clara MacCarald, *Monsters and Creatures of World Mythology*. San Diego, CA: BrightPoint Press, 2023.

June Smalls, *Celtic Gods, Heroes, and Mythology*. Minneapolis, MN: Abdo Publishing, 2019.

INTERNET SOURCES

"Ancient Egyptian Gods and Goddesses," *DK Find Out!*, 2022. www.dkfindout.com.

"The Gods and Goddesses of Ancient Greece!" *National Geographic Kids*, n.d. www.natgeokids.com.

"Myths and Archetypes," *PBS*, n.d. www.pbs.org.

WEBSITES

Discovering Ancient Egypt
https://discoveringegypt.com

Discovering Ancient Egypt includes stories about ancient Egyptian gods, as well as maps and drawings related to this civilization's mythology.

Greek Mythology
www.greekmythology.com

Greek Mythology includes a set of stories about the gods, goddesses, and heroes of the ancient Greeks.

Mythopedia
https://mythopedia.com

Mythopedia offers more than 200 articles about mythology from nine different cultures. The site aims to educate and entertain readers with its content.

INDEX

afterlife, 46–54
Anansi, 28–29
Aphrodite, 35–37, 39
Athena, 42–43, 45

Campbell, Joseph, 34, 38
creation, 10–11, 12–21, 51

Daiiru, 19
death, 10–11, 46–48, 52–54

Epic of Gilgamesh, 9
Eros, 34–35, 37, 38–39

fire, 30–31
floods, 6, 9–10

growth, 26–27

Hermes, 40
hero's journey, 10–11, 32–45

immortality, 8, 24, 26
Izanagi, 15
Izanami, 15

Karusakaibö, 19

Maui, 20–21
Medusa, 40, 41
Monkey King, 22–26, 27

Nyame, 29

Odin, 16–17
Opossum, 30–31
Osiris, 54

Pangu, 13–15
Persephone, 37
Perseus, 40–45
Psyche, 34–39

Quetzacóatl, 48–51

Ragnarok, 54–57
rebirth, 57
religion, 14

tricksters, 10–11, 22–31

Utnapishtim, 6–7, 8

Ymir, 16–19

IMAGE CREDITS

Cover: © Delcarmat/Shutterstock Images
5: © Rudall 30/Shutterstock Images
7: © Ivy Close Images/Alamy
9: © Swongpiriyaporn/iStockphoto
11: © Johan Swanepoel/Shutterstock Images
13: © Mike Pellinni/Shutterstock Images
17: © Chronicle/Alamy
18: © Svetlana Foote/Shutterstock Images
21: © Shane Myers Photography/Shutterstock Images
23: © Delcarmat/Shutterstock Images
25: © Bundit Yuwannasiri/Shutterstock Images
28: © Ondrej Chvatal/Shutterstock Images
31: © Filo/iStockphoto
33: © Alex Tooth/Shutterstock Images
35: © Album/Alamy
36: © Ivy Close Images/Alamy
41: © Rudall 30/Shutterstock Images
42: © Sergey Mikhaylov/iStockphoto
44: © Seamuss/Shutterstock Images
47: © JC Gonram/Shutterstock Images
49: © Clicks de Mexico/Shutterstock Images
53: © Zvereva Yana/Shutterstock Images
55: © Mitch Boeck/Shutterstock Images
56: © Charles Walker Collection/Alamy

ABOUT THE AUTHOR

Rebecca van den Ham writes for children and teens. She loves anything that begins with "Once upon a time." She lives with her family in Southern California, where she creates with words, paper, and fabric. She recommends visiting the library every week.